Published by UTU Media® - © 2026 Bridget Irby

ISBN - 9781966130031
Unless indicated otherwise, all Scriptures marked KJV are taken from the KING JAMES VERSION (KJV): KING JAMES VERSION, public domain.
Printed in the United States of America

Dear Reader,
This Book Is Dedicated To You.

*Your journey may not always be easy but, it is worth it.
I pray you find the words inside helpful and healing.*

Have you ever felt it? That gentle whisper in your heart telling you that God has so much more for your life? That there's a deeper relationship with Him waiting just around the corner, if only you knew how to get there?

Maybe you're doing all the "right" things. You're reading your Bible (or at least trying to), showing up to church (most Sundays), and praying (even if sometimes it feels like your prayers are hitting the ceiling and bouncing right back). Yet somehow, it feels like you're stuck in spiritual quicksand – the more you struggle, the deeper you sink.

Here's the truth: Sometimes, the path to more of God isn't about doing more things right – **it's about stopping the things that are holding you back**.

This is exactly why I created the "You Are Not Called" series. These books aren't about adding more to your spiritual to-do list. Instead, they're about gaining freedom by doing less – freedom from anxiety that steals your peace, freedom from fear that holds you captive, freedom from anger that robs your joy, freedom from shame that keeps you hidden, and freedom from loneliness that makes you feel disconnected from God and others.

I'm not writing these books from some lofty spiritual mountaintop. I'm writing as someone who has crawled through the valleys of anxiety, fear, anger, shame, and loneliness – and discovered that God was there all along, waiting to show me a better way. As an ordained minister, yes, but more importantly, as a woman who has lived every word on these pages, I can tell you with absolute certainty: You are not called to live this way. You are not called to be anxious, afraid, angry, ashamed, or alone. These struggles are not your inheritance as a child of God.

Think of this series as your spiritual "stop it" list. Just like a gardener needs to pull out weeds before planting new seeds, we need to identify and remove the things that are choking our spiritual growth.

I've seen God's transformative power firsthand. Each book in this series represents a battle I've fought and won, not through my own strength, but through discovering what God says about who we are and what we're called to be.

This journey won't always be easy but I promise you this: if you're ready to let go of what's holding you back, if you're willing to challenge the lies you've believed, and if you're prepared to step into the freedom God has for you, your life will never be the same. Because the truth is, sister, you were created for more than just surviving – you were created to thrive.

With faith, hope, and a whole lot of grace,

Christian Friends Are The Best Friends!

There are moments in life when loneliness feels like it's closing in from every direction. Not the quiet kind of alone that brings rest, but the heavy kind that settles into your chest and makes everything feel harder — breathing, thinking, hoping. Sometimes loneliness shows up after heartbreak. Sometimes after disappointment. Sometimes after transition. And sometimes, it just appears, even when you're surrounded by people.

I've lived in that kind of loneliness. I've sat in rooms full of noise and still felt unseen. I've been in seasons where I didn't know who to trust, where to lean, or how to ask for help. And if you're holding this book, I want you to hear this with gentleness and truth:

Loneliness is not who you are.
 It is not your identity.
 It is not your forever.
 And it is not a sign that something is wrong with you.

You were created for connection — deep, safe, God-centered connection. But life has a way of pulling us away from what we were made for. Hurt hardens us. Disappointment distances us. Fear isolates us. And slowly, loneliness becomes the air we breathe.

But not anymore.

This study is your invitation back into the life God designed for you — one where you are surrounded, supported, strengthened, and known. You will uproot lies, break unhealthy patterns, rebuild trust, and open your heart again. You'll learn to connect — not from fear or striving, but from identity and wholeness.

I pray that as you walk through these pages, you feel God sitting with you... speaking to you... guiding you back into the community He has prepared for you.

You are not called to be alone.
 You are called to belong.

Let's rebuild together.

Lots of Love,
Bridget

xoxo

Hey Friend,

Before you begin, I want to say this as clearly as possible: I see you, and I get it.

Walking through loneliness — especially as a woman who loves God, carries responsibility, and pours into everyone else — can feel confusing and painful. We're often taught to be strong, to push through, to keep going. But strength without support becomes survival, not living.

That's why I wrote this study.

Not from a place of theory...
but from a place of experience.
Not from a pedestal...
but from the same valleys you've walked through.
Not as someone who "figured it out"...
but as someone who let God rebuild her piece by piece.

Over these eight weeks, you will feel challenged, encouraged, convicted, stretched, and comforted. There may be moments where emotions rise unexpectedly — let them. Healing doesn't always look neat, but it does look holy.

Each lesson is crafted to move you gently but powerfully from loneliness to connection, from isolation to community, from guarded to grounded, from surviving to belonging.

You are stepping into something new.
Something light.
Something whole.
Something connected.

And I'm honored to walk it with you.

love you,
Bridget

Free Resources

Hey there, superstar!

I'm so proud of you for starting this journey and because I'm not about to send you out there empty-handed, I've got some awesome resources to help you on your journey.

Think of these as your toolkit. They're like the Swiss Army knife of emotional and spiritual growth - versatile, handy, and they might just save you in a pinch (though maybe don't try to use them to open a can or cut down a small tree).

To access the resources, simply create your free account at www.youarenotcalled.com.

Inside, you'll have to the above resources plus much more!

A Not-So-Boring-But-Very-Important Disclaimer

(Please Read This, Even If You Usually Skip These Things)

Before we dive into this adventure together, we need to have a little chat. You know, the kind that usually comes with a cup of coffee and a "Now, don't freak out, but..." opener. So, grab your beverage of choice (I won't judge if it's not coffee), and let's get real for a moment.

First things first: I am not a doctor, therapist, counselor, or any other type of licensed mental health professional. I know, shocking right? Despite my incredible ability to dispense wisdom and wit (if I do say so myself), my qualifications are more in the realm of "life experience" and "passionate Jesus follower" than "Ph.D. in Psychology."

This book, as awesome as it is (and trust me, it's pretty awesome), is not meant to replace the invaluable work of trained professionals. Think of it more as a heart-to-heart with a friend who's been there, done that, and got the t-shirt (and maybe a few therapy sessions) to prove it.

If you're dealing with severe anger issues, depression, anxiety, or any other mental health concerns, **please, please, PLEASE seek help from a qualified professional.** They have tools in their toolbox that go way beyond what I can offer here. *(Plus, they probably have comfier couches for you to sit on while you talk.)*

This book is meant to be a companion on your journey, not your only guide. It's like having a workout buddy – super helpful and motivating, but not a substitute for a trained physical therapist if you've got a serious injury.

So, if at any point while reading this book you think, "Wow, I could really use some professional help with this," then congratulations! You've just had an incredibly mature and self-aware moment. Seriously, give yourself a pat on the back, then go find yourself a therapist. Your future self will thank you.

Remember, seeking help is not a sign of weakness. It's a sign that you're brave enough to admit you don't have all the answers (welcome to the club, by the way) and smart enough to ask for guidance. That's the kind of wisdom that would make Solomon proud!

Now, with all that said, I truly believe that this book has the potential to be a powerful tool in your spiritual and emotional growth journey. Just think of it as one piece of your "becoming-the-best-version-of-yourself" puzzle, not the whole picture.

So, are we clear? This book = awesome friend and spiritual cheerleader. Trained professionals = necessary allies for serious stuff. You = amazing child of God who deserves all the help and support you can get.

Alright, now that we've got that out of the way, let's get back to the good stuff. You've got a life-changing journey ahead of you, and I, for one, can't wait to see where it takes you. Just remember, if the road gets too bumpy, don't be afraid to call in some professional reinforcements. After all, even Batman needed Alfred, right?

Remember...

There's no rush.

You and me, love, we've got our whole lives to figure this thing out. Don't let rushing steal your joy.

There's no wrong answer.

This is unique to you and you simply cannot get it wrong. Just be honest with yourself and we can go from there.

You are doing great.

High five sister! Just the fact that you are here, with God, working on you says everything. Congratulations!

Week One

Day 1: You Were Created For Connection

Before sin entered the world, before brokenness existed, before fear ever whispered its first lie — God declared something "not good."

And it wasn't darkness.
It wasn't chaos.
It wasn't temptation.
It was aloneness.

God looked at Adam standing in perfection — a garden full of provision, beauty, purpose, and direct access to God Himself — and He still said, "This is not good."

If Adam wasn't designed to live alone in paradise, Sis… why would you be expected to live alone in a fallen world?

Connection is God's idea.
Community is God's strategy.
Relationship is God's design.

Loneliness feels heavy because it contradicts how you were created. It's like trying to run a marathon on a broken ankle — you can try, but it will hurt with every step.

You were created with:
· a mind that needs encouragement
· a heart that needs support
· a spirit that needs sharpening
· a body that needs rest
· emotions that need safe places

Isolation starves what God intended to be nourished through people.

Hear me:
Needing people is not weakness. It's design.

The enemy whispers, "You don't need anyone."
God whispers, "You were never meant to carry this alone."

One isolates.
One heals.

READ GENESIS 2:18 (KJV)

Spend time praying right now that God reveal
to you where the enemy is attacking your mind.
Where in your life have you been carrying
something alone? Journal your thoughts below.

Tell God out loud: "Father, I was created for connection. Show me where I've embraced isolation instead of community."

Our culture loves the idea of "I don't need anybody."
Be strong.
Be independent.
Handle it alone.
Prove you can manage everything without support.

But independence — when taken to the extreme — becomes a prison disguised as strength.

Ecclesiastes 4:9–10 says, "Two are better than one... if either of them falls, one can help the other up."

Not "two are helpful."
Not "two are convenient."
Two are better.
Because God never intended for you to be the only one holding up your life.

Some of us didn't choose independence — independence was forced on us.
You became strong because someone dropped you.
You learned to survive because no one showed up for you.
You raised yourself emotionally because no one taught you how to need people safely.

But survival-mode strength is not God's best for you.

God wants to take you from:
· self-protection → healthy vulnerability
· self-reliance → supported living
· emotional isolation → spiritual connection
· carrying everything → sharing the weight

Needing people doesn't make you weak — it makes you human.

And letting people in doesn't make you fragile — it makes you free.

Sis, independence is not your identity.
It was a coping mechanism.
And God is inviting you into a better way.

Bible Reading

READ ECCLESIASTES 4:9–10
(KJV)

Read the scripture, then spend time in prayer asking God to reveal to you where independence has been a shield, and where it has become a prison?

Today's Challenge

Ask God to soften one area where you've relied only on yourself.

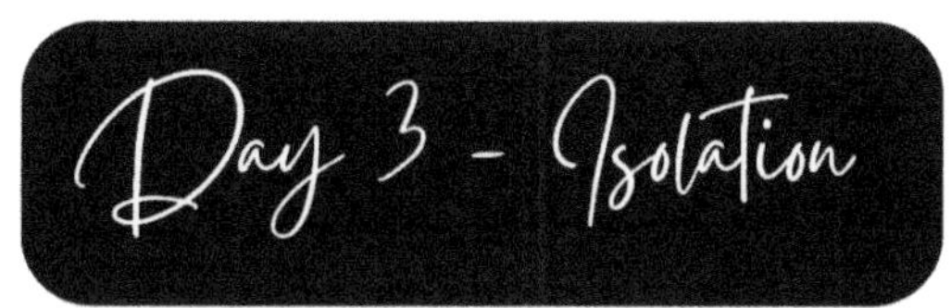

The enemy's favorite battlefield is isolation.
When you're alone, your thoughts are louder.
Lies are more convincing.
Fear feels heavier.
Discouragement hits deeper.
Temptation becomes stronger.

1 Peter 5:8 warns us: "Your enemy the devil prowls around like a roaring lion looking for someone to devour."

Do you know how a lion attacks?
It separates the prey from the herd.
Once alone, the prey becomes vulnerable — not because it's weak, but because it is unprotected.

This is exactly why the enemy pushes you toward isolation:
He knows you're easier to attack when you're alone.
He knows your thoughts spiral faster when you're alone.
He knows fear multiplies quicker when you're alone.

Isolation is spiritual strategy — and not God's.

The enemy whispers:
• "No one understands."
• "You'll be judged."
• "You're too much."
• "Handle it yourself."
• "People always leave."

Those lies aren't random — they are intentional.

But Jesus calls you into connection, protection, and community because He knows where your strength is multiplied.

You are harder to attack when someone is praying for you.
You are harder to deceive when someone is speaking truth over you.
You are harder to isolate when someone is checking in on you.
You are harder to discourage when someone sits with you in your pain.

Bible Reading

READ 1 PETER 5:8 (KJV)

What lie has isolation whispered to you most recently? Take some time to pray over this scripture with a heart that seeks God's will and clarity. Journal your thoughts and answers below.

Speak this out loud today: "Isolation is not my portion. Connection is my calling."

Day 4 - You Were Created To be Supported

Psalm 68:6 reveals something powerful about God's heart:
He doesn't just comfort the lonely — He places them.
He connects them.
He surrounds them.
He sets them into community.

Loneliness isn't a flaw.
It's a signal.
It's your soul saying, "I wasn't built for this."

God designed you to:
· be seen
· be heard
· be supported
· be understood
· be prayed for
· be surrounded

You were created to thrive in connection, not survive in isolation.

One of the greatest lies of loneliness is:
"Everyone has someone except me."

But Sis, hear me — that is not truth.
You are not the exception to belonging.
You are not disqualified from connection.
You are not destined to walk life alone.

There are relationships God is preparing for you.
There are people who will love you well.
There are safe spaces you haven't stepped into yet.
There are women who will hold your arms up when you're tired.
There are friendships that will heal wounds you didn't know you still carried.

God isn't finished writing your community story.

Bible Reading

READ PSALM 68:6 (KJV)

What do you think today's reading means in the context of your life? What part of being known feels the scariest — and why? Journal your thoughts below after reading and spending time in prayer.

Today's Challenge

Pray this: "Lord, set me into the community You've prepared for me. Give me courage to step into connection."

Weekly Recap

This week was a gentle but powerful reminder that you were never created for isolation. You were created for connection — not optional connection, but essential connection. God designed your heart to be strengthened through people, encouraged through relationship, protected through community, and surrounded by those who will lift you up when life feels too heavy to carry alone.

Reflect on what God highlighted within you this week:
· Where have you been carrying life by yourself?
· Where has independence become a shield instead of strength?
· What lies has isolation whispered to you?
· Where is God inviting you back into community?
· Who might God be preparing to walk with you?

Take a moment to acknowledge this truth:
Loneliness does not mean you're forgotten.
It means your heart is longing for what God designed you for.

This week wasn't about fixing loneliness — it was about understanding your design. And once you understand your design, you can start to align your life with it.

Let God soften what isolation hardened.
Let Him heal what loneliness tried to define.
Let Him guide you gently back into the relationships He has prepared for you.

You are not alone.
God is with you — and He is bringing people to surround you.

Weekly Prayer

Father,
  Thank you for creating me for connection, not isolation.

  Show me where I've been carrying life alone and teach me to lean into the relationships You have prepared for me.

  Heal the places where independence became a shield and soften the walls I've built around my heart.

  Protect my mind from loneliness and guide me into safe, God-appointed community.

  Remind me daily that I am seen, known, and supported.

In Jesus' name,
  Amen.

Week Two

Most loneliness begins with a wound — a moment that broke your trust, your safety, or your sense of belonging. It might've been a betrayal, a loss, a rejection, a relationship ending, or a season where support fell apart when you needed it most. But regardless of what caused it, here's the truth:

Loneliness often starts the moment your heart breaks... and you don't have anyone safe to catch the pieces.

Psalm 34:18 tells us that God is close to the brokenhearted — not after you heal, not after you recover, not after you "get over it." He draws near in the breaking, in the place where loneliness first entered.

Loneliness isn't just the absence of people.
Loneliness is the absence of feeling supported.

And when your heart is wounded, it becomes harder to let others close. You stop trusting easily. You pull back. You decide you'll depend on yourself because you don't want to feel abandoned again.

The wound wasn't your fault.
The withdrawal wasn't your intention.
But the loneliness became your reality.

Today is about recognizing that the root isn't your weakness — it's your wound.

WRITE OUT PSALM 34:18 (KJV)

Journal Prompt:

What past wound do you feel most
connected to your loneliness?

Tell God honestly: "Here is the wound I've been carrying alone."
Speak it out loud.

Loneliness often grows in the gap between what you hoped for and what actually happened. Proverbs 13:12 says, "Hope deferred makes the heart sick." When expectations are unmet, the heart doesn't just ache — it shuts down.

Sometimes loneliness starts with disappointment that slowly turns into distance:

· A friend didn't show up when you needed them
· The relationship you prayed for fell apart
· Someone made promises they never kept
· A community you trusted hurt you
· A season you hoped would bring connection brought separation instead

Disappointment teaches the heart a dangerous lesson:
"Lower your expectations."

So you stop expecting people to stay.
You stop expecting depth.
You stop expecting support.
You stop expecting to be understood.
And eventually... you stop expecting connection altogether.

But the heart that stops expecting connection begins to live in isolation — not because it wants to be alone, but because it's afraid of being let down again.

Let me sit with you in this:
Your disappointment is valid.
Your heartache is real.
And God sees the distance that formed because of it.

But He also wants you to know:
Disappointment is where the hurt started — not where the story ends.

Bible Reading

Journal Prompt:

What disappointment has quietly shaped
your heart's distance?

Today's Challenge

Write the phrase: "My disappointment is not the end of my connection story."

Guarding your heart is biblical — but guarding it too tightly becomes harmful. Proverbs 4:23 says to guard your heart, but many of us build walls instead of gates.

Walls keep everything out — even what God wants to let in.
Gates let wisdom in, but keep danger out.

Loneliness often takes root when self-protection becomes overprotection. It starts innocently:
"I don't want to be hurt again."
"I can't handle another betrayal."
"I need to be careful this time."
"I'm better off staying to myself."

But slowly, that caution turns into isolation.
You stop opening up.
You stop reaching out.
You avoid deep conversations.
You keep things surface-level.
You convince yourself you're "fine" alone — even when you're not.

Self-protection feels safe, but it becomes a trap when it keeps your heart from receiving the love, support, and community God sends to heal you.

Here's the truth:
You didn't build walls because you're difficult — you built them because you were hurting.
But you don't have to keep living behind them.

Healing begins the moment you realize your walls kept you safe once — but now, they're keeping you lonely.

Bible Reading

READ, REFLECT, & PRAY ON
PROVERBS 4:23 (KJV)

Journal Prompt:

Where have you built walls instead of

gates?

Today's Challenge

Ask God: "Show me one wall I can begin lowering with Your help."

Overwhelm doesn't just exhaust you — it isolates you.

When life becomes too heavy, too chaotic, or too painful, hiding feels easier than connecting. You withdraw not because you don't want people... but because you don't have the capacity for them.

Loneliness rooted in overwhelm often sounds like this:
"I don't want to be a burden."
"I don't even know how to explain what I'm feeling."
"I don't have the energy for people."
"I don't want to cry in front of anyone."
"I'll handle it myself."

But Psalm 61:2 says, "When my heart is overwhelmed, lead me to the Rock that is higher than I."

Notice it doesn't say:
"When my heart is overwhelmed, handle it alone."

God doesn't call you to hide — He calls you to lean.
But overwhelm tricks you into thinking pulling away will protect you.

It doesn't.
It isolates you.
And isolation intensifies the overwhelm.

Overwhelm is not a sign that you're weak.
It's a sign that you're carrying something too heavy by yourself.

God wants to strengthen you — not in solitude, but in support.

Bible Reading

**READ, REFLECT, & PRAY ON
PSALM 61:2 (KJV)**

Journal Prompt:

Where has overwhelm caused you to pull
away from others?

Today's Challenge

Tell God one area that feels too heavy to carry alone.

Weekly Recap

This week, you uncovered something many people never stop to examine: the roots of loneliness. You learned that loneliness isn't random, and it isn't a personal flaw. It grows where wounds haven't healed, disappointments haven't been processed, walls haven't been lowered, and overwhelm hasn't been shared.

Pause and reflect on what God revealed:
· Which wound shaped your loneliness more than you realized?
· Where did disappointment create distance?
· What walls have you built to feel safe?
· How has overwhelm pushed you into hiding?
· Where did you feel God's nearness this week?

Loneliness is not a sign that something is wrong with you.
It is a sign that something happened to you — and God is bringing healing to those places.
He is uncovering roots so He can restore them.
He is revealing wounds so He can heal them.
He is softening your heart so it can reconnect again.

This week wasn't about fixing loneliness — it was about understanding it. And when something is understood, it loses its power to shame you. You don't have to hide from your loneliness anymore. You can bring it into the light, where God transforms it.

Let this truth settle over you:
Your loneliness is not your identity — it is a chapter God is rewriting into healing.

Dear Father,

Thank you for revealing the roots of my loneliness with gentleness and truth.

Heal the wounds that opened the door to isolation.

Restore the places where disappointment, overwhelm, or fear built walls around my heart.

Help me tear down the barriers that keep me from connection and guide me into the relationships You've prepared for me.

Teach me to trust again and lead me into deeper healing every day.

In Jesus' name,
Amen.

Week Three

One of the most damaging lies loneliness whispers is this:
"There must be something wrong with me."

When connection feels distant or relationships feel inconsistent, you begin to wonder if you're the common denominator. You may replay past conversations, analyze old friendships, or critique pieces of your personality you once loved. Loneliness convinces you that your worth is based on who stays, who notices, or who reaches out.

But Psalm 139:14 confronts this lie with bold truth:
You are fearfully and wonderfully made — intentionally, specifically, beautifully, purposefully.
Your identity is not defined by who didn't choose you.
Your value is not measured by who didn't show up.
Your worth is not determined by how many people are in your life right now.

You are not "too much."
You are not "not enough."
You are not unworthy, unlovable, or undesirable.

The absence of people is not the evidence of something wrong with you — it's the evidence of seasons, transitions, wounds, timing, and the normal complexities of life. Loneliness tries to make it personal, but God makes it purposeful.

You're not broken.
You're becoming.
You're not defective.
You're developing.

Loneliness is loud — but lies always are.

READ, REFLECT, & PRAY ON
PSALM 139:14 (KJV)

Journal Prompt:

Where have you internalized the idea

that "something must be wrong with

me"?

Today's Challenge

Speak this aloud: "There is nothing wrong with me. I am fearfully and wonderfully made."

Loneliness often twists reality into one painful belief:
"No one cares."

It's not that no one cares — it's that you haven't felt cared for in the ways your heart needed. And when care doesn't look how you expected, the enemy uses disappointment to convince you you're forgotten.

But here's the truth:
People care in different ways, with different capacities, from different levels of emotional maturity.
Just because care is inconsistent doesn't mean it's absent.
Just because one person failed you doesn't mean everyone will.
Just because someone didn't show up doesn't mean you aren't deeply valued.

And even when people fall short — God never does.
1 Peter 5:7 says God cares for you — intentionally, constantly, personally.

God cares:
· about the details you think are too small
· about the pain you think is too dramatic
· about the fears you think are too embarrassing
· about the dreams you think are too big
· about the tears you cried alone in your car
· about the moments no one saw

Care that comes from God is steady.
Care that comes from God is unconditional.
Care that comes from God is not based on convenience.

You are cared for — deeply — even when you feel alone.

Bible Reading

Journal Prompt:

Where have you equated feeling uncared

for with being uncared for?

Today's Challenge

Pray: "Lord, show me the ways You care for me every day."

One of the harshest lies loneliness speaks is the lie of unbelonging:
"I don't fit anywhere."

Maybe you've walked into rooms where you didn't feel seen.
Maybe you tried to connect with people who didn't reciprocate.
Maybe you've outgrown old circles but haven't found new ones yet.
Maybe you've changed, but the people around you haven't.
Maybe your faith isolated you from old friendships.
Maybe your growth created distance.

And slowly, you began to believe you're the "extra piece in the puzzle," the one who doesn't fit the picture.

But Ephesians 2:19 says the exact opposite:
You ARE part of God's household.
You DO belong.
You ARE connected.
You ARE included.
You ARE chosen.

Belonging isn't something you earn — it's something God ordains.

Sometimes God pulls you out of old circles so He can place you in new ones. Sometimes you don't fit because the room was too small for your calling. Sometimes you feel disconnected because God is preparing a community that matches your growth, your heart, your healing, and your purpose.

You don't belong "nowhere."
You belong somewhere God is preparing.

Bible Reading

Journal Prompt:

Where have you felt the sting of not belonging?

Declare: "My belonging comes from God, not from people."

Loneliness feels permanent.
It convinces you that nothing will change, that connection won't come, and that you're stuck in a season you can't get out of.

The enemy loves to say:
"This is just who you are now."
"This is your life."
"This is your story."
"This is all you get."

But Isaiah 43:19 interrupts that lie with a powerful declaration:
"See, I am doing a new thing… do you not perceive it?"

God is always moving in places you cannot see.
Doors are being prepared.
Relationships are being aligned.
Healing is happening beneath the surface.
Restoration is in progress.
Your story is still unfolding.

Loneliness isn't your identity — it's your season.
And seasons are temporary.

You are not stuck.
You are not forgotten.
You are not destined for isolation.
You are in the middle of a transition — and transitions always feel lonely.

Let this truth settle over your heart:
God is not finished with your story.
Newness is coming.
Connection is coming.
Healing is coming.
Community is coming.

Your story is not over — it is evolving.

READ, REFLECT, & PRAY ON
ISAIAH 43:19 (KJV)

Journal Prompt:

Where have you believed loneliness will

always be part of your story?

Today's Challenge

Speak: "God is doing a new thing in my life. My story is changing."

Weekly Recap

This week you confronted the lies loneliness has been whispering — the lies that shape how you see yourself, how you interpret your relationships, and how you believe God sees you. These lies feel real because they often echo past experiences, not present truth. But now, you're learning to recognize the difference.

Reflect on what stood out this week:
• Has loneliness made you believe something is wrong with you?
• Have you mistaken lack of communication for lack of care?
• Have you convinced yourself you don't belong anywhere?
• Have you believed loneliness is permanent?

These lies are not your truth.
They are not your destiny.
They are not your identity.

This week wasn't about pretending loneliness doesn't exist — it was about refusing to let loneliness define your worth. Lies lose their power the moment they are exposed... and replaced with truth.

Let the truth settle into your spirit:
You are valuable.
You are cared for.
You are placed by God.
You are in a season — not a life sentence.

As you continue this study, remember:
Loneliness may speak, but God gets the final word.

Weekly Prayer

Dear Lord,

Thank You for revealing the lies loneliness has spoken over my life.

Replace every false belief with Your truth.

Remind me of my worth, my belonging, and the love You have for me.

Heal the places where lies took root and renew my mind with Your Word.

Help me recognize Your voice above every whisper of loneliness.

Strengthen my heart to believe that my story is not over and that You are doing a new thing in my life.

In Jesus' name,
Amen.

Week Four

Connection begins with an open heart — but opening your heart again after hurt feels risky. Sometimes, it feels impossible. You may want connection, yet feel protective. You may crave closeness, yet fear being misunderstood, rejected, or disappointed again. This tension doesn't mean you're weak — it means you're human.

Ezekiel 36:26 promises that God can give you a new heart — not a harder one, not a guarded one, not a self-protected one… but a renewed one. A soft heart that can receive love again. A healed heart that can trust again. A strengthened heart that can connect again.

Here's the truth:
Your heart doesn't reopen all at once. It opens one small moment at a time.
A conversation.
A shared truth.
A tiny step of honesty.
A willingness to be seen.

Connection doesn't require perfection — it requires presence.
You don't have to pour your heart out on day one. You just have to open one door, one inch.

Ask yourself: Where is God inviting my heart to soften?
Not where you should perform.
Not where you should force.
Just where He's gently nudging.

Bible Reading

READ EZEKIEL 36:26 (KJV)

Spend time praying right now that God reveals to you what part of your heart is the most guarded right now? Journal your thoughts below.

Today's Challenge

Whisper this truth: "God, soften my heart where it has been closed."

Trust is complicated. You've been hurt. You've been let down. You've had people mishandle your heart, your story, your vulnerability. So naturally, trust feels dangerous. But trust doesn't mean being naïve — trust means allowing your heart to breathe again.

Proverbs 3:5 doesn't tell you to trust people blindly — it tells you to trust God. Because when your ultimate trust is in God, you can trust people with clearer eyes. Wisdom protects you from unsafe connections, but fear prevents you from any connections.

Healthy trust sounds like this:

• "I can share gently and at my pace."

• "I can build trust layer by layer."

• "I can use discernment without shutting down."

• "I can let people into safe parts of my life."

• "I can trust God to protect me as I open up."

You're not relearning trust in a vacuum — you're relearning trust with God guiding each step.

The enemy says, "Don't trust anyone."

God says, "Trust Me first — and I'll show you who is safe."

Bible Reading

Read the scripture, then spend time in prayer asking God to reveal to you where you have confused wisdom with fear.

Today's Challenge

Pray: "God, teach me to trust wisely, not fearfully."

Day 3 - Building God-Aligned Connections

Connection is beautiful — but not every connection is healthy. One of the biggest steps in healing loneliness is learning how to identify relationships that are aligned with who you are becoming, not who you used to be.

Amos 3:3 reminds us that for two people to walk together, they must be in agreement — that means shared values, mutual respect, emotional safety, and spiritual alignment. Some of your loneliness has nothing to do with you; it's because you were yoked to people who didn't match your heart, your calling, or your growth.

Healthy connections are:
- reciprocal, not one-sided
- life-giving, not draining
- supportive, not competitive
- honest, not manipulative
- spiritually aligned, not spiritually conflicting

When God brings people into your life, it feels like peace — not chaos. It feels like clarity — not confusion. It feels like alignment — not compromise.

You don't have to force connection with people who don't have the capacity for you. And you don't have to cling to relationships God is gently releasing.

Ask: Does this relationship pull me closer to God, or farther from Him? Healthy connection always leads you upward.

Bible Reading

READ AMOS 3:3 (KJV)

Which relationships in your life feel aligned with your growth — and which ones don't? Take some time to pray over this scripture with a heart that seeks God's will and clarity. Journal your thoughts and answers below.

Today's Challenge

Write: "Lord, align my relationships with Your purpose for me."

Day 4 – Taking Steps Into Community

Healing from loneliness is not just internal — it's relational. But stepping into community after a season of isolation requires courage. Not reckless courage, not rushed courage — brave but safe courage.

Hebrews 10:24–25 urges us not to forsake gathering but to encourage one another. But "gathering" doesn't just mean showing up in a room — it means allowing yourself to engage, to connect, to be part of something again.

Your first steps don't have to be dramatic.
You don't need to join every group.
You don't need to spill your life story on day one.
You don't need to force instant intimacy.

Your brave steps can be small:
· saying yes to one invitation
· joining one group
· sending one message
· staying five minutes longer
· sharing one truth about your day
· asking someone how they're really doing

Community grows slowly and intentionally — not instantly.

You're not returning to community as the same person who left. You're returning wiser. Softer. Stronger. More grounded.

And God will guide your steps, leading you into rooms where you'll be received, not rejected.

Bible Reading

READ HEBREWS 10:24–25
(KJV)

What do you think today's reading means in the context of your life? What is one "brave but safe" step you can take toward community this week? Journal your thoughts below after reading and spending time in prayer.

Today's Challenge

Commit to taking that step within the next 72 hours.

Weekly Recap

This week wasn't about forcing connection — it was about relearning it. You acknowledged that connection doesn't automatically feel easy after loneliness. You learned to open your heart gently, trust wisely, identify aligned relationships, and take courageous steps into community.

Reflect on what stood out:

· What part of your heart is God softening?

· Where is He teaching you wisdom instead of fear?

· What does a healthy, aligned connection look like for you now?

· What practical steps is He nudging you to take?

You are in a transformation season — and transformation always requires new skills. Connection is a practice, not a personality trait. And every small step you take brings you closer to the relationships God has prepared for you.

Let this truth settle in you:

You are capable of connection.

You are safe to open up again.

You are becoming someone who builds healthy, God-centered relationships.

You are moving toward community, not away from it.

Connection is not beyond you — it is being rebuilt within you.

Weekly Prayer

Dear Father,

Thank you for gently teaching me how to reconnect.

Heal the places where fear and past hurt have kept my heart closed.

Give me wisdom to trust wisely and courage to take steps toward community.

Align me with people who honor You and encourage my growth.

Help me walk into new relationships with confidence, clarity, and emotional safety.

Continue softening my heart and guiding my steps as I relearn connection.

In Jesus' name,
Amen.

Week Five

Day 1: Learning God's Design For Community

To understand God-centered community, look at the early church in Acts 2. They devoted themselves to fellowship. Not casually attended. Not "showed up when convenient." Devoted. Connected. Committed.

Community is part of God's blueprint for the Christian life. It's where you are strengthened, sharpened, encouraged, prayed for, and held accountable. It's where you grow spiritually and emotionally. It's where purpose is confirmed, gifts are activated, and healing takes root.

God's design for community has four pillars:

1. Shared faith — Common belief creates common ground.

2. Shared purpose — Growing toward Christ together.

3. Shared responsibility — Everyone contributes to the relationship.

4. Shared care — Support flows both ways.

Loneliness begins to break when you understand that community is not optional — it's essential.

And the community God is preparing for you will not require you to shrink, hide, overperform, or pretend. It will feel like alignment. It will feel like being known. It will feel like home.

You're not too much for the right community.
You're not too emotional, too busy, too spiritual, too quiet, or too wounded.
You are exactly who God designed — and the right people will see that.

READ ACTS 2:42 (KJV)

Spend time praying right now that God reveal to you and answer this. How have you viewed community — as optional or essential?

Pray: "God, teach me what community should look like in my life."

You don't need more people — you need the right people.
People who are wise. People who love God. People who sharpen you. People who carry peace. People who point you back to Christ. People who walk with integrity. People who value emotional health. People who are consistent, not chaotic.

Proverbs 13:20 reminds us that who you walk with shapes who you become. Your community influences your thoughts, your decisions, your faith, your healing, and your direction.

God-centered people:
· speak life into you
· protect your purpose
· encourage your growth
· correct you with love
· celebrate your wins
· pray over your battles
· carry wisdom, not drama

You don't have to force yourself into relationships that drain you.
You don't have to tolerate inconsistency to avoid being alone.
You don't have to settle for proximity — God wants alignment.

And hear me clearly:
You are not behind.
You are not "late to the party."
You are not too old, too busy, too wounded, or too disconnected to find your people.

God is not going to surround you with "just anyone."
He is preparing people who are emotionally mature enough to handle you and spiritually grounded enough to walk with you.

READ PROVERBS 13:20 (KJV)

Read the scripture, then spend time in prayer asking God to reveal to you wisdom, and then answer this. What qualities do you want in God-centered people?

Today's Challenge

Write a list of 5 non-negotiable traits for the relationships God is
bringing into your life.

Healthy community requires healthy people — people who not only receive love, but give it. Being part of a God-centered community means learning how to be a safe person for others, too.

A safe person is:
- consistent, not unpredictable
- honest, not passive-aggressive
- honoring, not gossiping
- empathetic, not dismissive
- trustworthy, not careless
- patient, not reactive
- Christ-like, not self-focused

Romans 12:10 says to be devoted to one another in love — devotion means showing up for people not only in convenience, but in compassion, patience, and truth.

Being a safe person doesn't mean you fix everyone. It means you:
- listen well
- pray sincerely
- hold confidences
- support without enabling
- encourage without rescuing
- care without carrying what isn't yours

This isn't about perfection — it's about posture.
The healthier you become, the healthier your community becomes.
The more you grow, the more you attract others who are growing.

Connection is not only about receiving — it's about contributing.
You are part of what God wants to build.

READ ROMANS 12:10 (KJV)

What quality of a "safe person" do you want to grow in? Take some time to pray over this scripture with a heart that seeks God's will and clarity. Journal your thoughts and answers below.

Today's Challenge

Pray: "Lord, make me a safe person for the community You are building in my life."

Community deepens through consistency, not intensity.
You don't need to be a perfect friend — you just need to be a present one.

Hebrews 10:24–25 reminds us to encourage one another and not give up meeting together. The early church didn't meet out of obligation — they met out of devotion. Rhythm builds relationship.

Consistency looks like:
· checking in
· following up
· showing up
· sending a prayer text
· having one honest conversation a week
· making space in your schedule
· building rituals with people
· engaging even when you're not at 100%

Consistency doesn't mean overextending yourself. It doesn't mean saying "yes" to everything. It means choosing connection on purpose — even in small ways.

Loneliness loses its power not just when you have people — but when you have rhythm with people.

Your goal isn't to find a hundred friends.
It's to cultivate deep, steady connection with a few God-aligned ones.

The right community grows slowly, intentionally, and prayerfully.

Bible Reading

READ HEBREWS 10:24–25 (KJV)

What do you think today's reading means in the context of your life? Where can you add more consistency to your connections? Journal your thoughts below after reading and spending time in prayer.

Today's Challenge

Choose one relationship and commit to one small consistent action this week.

Weekly Recap

This week you learned that building God-centered community isn't random — it's intentional. You saw what biblical community looks like, how to find the right people, how to show up as a safe person, and how consistency strengthens connection.

Reflect on what God highlighted:

· What part of God's design for community felt new to you?

· What qualities stood out in the kind of people you want in your life?

· Which traits do you want to cultivate in yourself?

· Where can you grow in consistency?

· What relationships is God nudging you to invest in?

You're not just healing loneliness — you're learning to build relationships that are healthy, reciprocal, aligned, and spiritually grounded. Community isn't about finding perfect people — it's about finding aligned people and being aligned yourself.

God is preparing a circle for you — a circle of support, prayer, encouragement, strength, and love. But He's also preparing you to be part of someone else's circle. Your growth is part of their blessing.

Let this truth sink in:

You are worthy of God-centered community.

You are ready for deeper, safer connections.

You are becoming the version of yourself who can hold and sustain healthy relationships.

You're not walking toward community alone — God is walking you right into it.

Weekly Prayer

Dear Father,

Thank You for showing me what God-centered community looks like.

Align me with the right people and teach me how to show up with wisdom, love, and grace.

Help me grow into a safe, consistent, Christ-centered friend.

Strengthen my heart to invest in the relationships You've prepared.

Guide me as I build rhythms of connection and surround me with people who reflect Your love.

Thank You for preparing a community that supports my growth and honors You.

In Jesus' name,
Amen.

Week Six

Healthy connection begins with emotional presence — the ability to check in, notice, respond, and be present for the people God has placed in your life.

Philippians 2:4 calls us to look beyond ourselves and genuinely care for others. This isn't a call to self-neglect — it's a call to shared emotional awareness. When you regularly check in with people, you create a rhythm of connection that keeps relationships from drifting.

But emotional presence also means checking in with yourself:

· How am I feeling today?
· Am I withdrawing?
· Am I overwhelmed?
· Am I overthinking?
· Am I expecting people to read my mind?

Relationships weaken silently long before they weaken loudly. Small emotional check-ins prevent big emotional breakdowns.

Establishing this rhythm means:
· Asking how someone is really doing
· Sending a voice note or encouragement
· Scheduling small touchpoints
· Updating loved ones instead of disappearing
· Communicating when you're not okay

You don't have to be emotionally perfect — just emotionally present.

READ PHILIPPIANS 2:4 (KJV)

Spend time praying right now that God reveals to you who in your life could benefit from a simple emotional check-in from you? Journal your thoughts below.

Today's Challenge

Send one heartfelt "How are you — really?" message today.

Honesty is the backbone of healthy relationships. Not honesty that wounds. Not honesty that explodes. Not honesty that avoids. Honesty that builds. Honesty that is grounded in love, clarity, and emotional maturity.

Ephesians 4:15 calls us to speak the truth in love — which means truth without harshness, and love without passivity.

Most relational tension comes from unspoken truth:
- "I didn't tell them that hurt me."
- "I didn't say I needed space."
- "I didn't admit I was overwhelmed."
- "I didn't share what I was feeling."
- "I didn't say I needed support."

Silence creates distance.
Avoidance creates confusion.
Assumptions create conflict.

Healthy rhythm means making honesty normal — not dramatic.
It means saying:
- "This bothered me, can we talk about it?"
- "I don't have capacity today."
- "I'm feeling disconnected."
- "I miss you."
- "I care about you, and I want to clear this up."

Honesty builds trust.
Honesty stabilizes emotions.
Honesty deepens connection.

You're not responsible for controlling people's reactions — only for communicating with love and clarity.

Bible Reading

READ EPHESIANS 4:15 (KJV)

Read the scripture, then spend time in prayer asking
God to reveal to you where in your relationships you have
held back truth that needed to be expressed.

Today's Challenge

Practice one honest — but gentle — sentence today.

Healthy relationships require rest — not just physical rest, but relational rest.

This means stepping back before burnout happens.

Taking breaks before resentment builds.

Saying "I need a moment" instead of withdrawing entirely.

Matthew 11:28 reminds us that rest comes from God — not isolation.

When you disconnect out of exhaustion instead of intention, loneliness grows.

When you rest with God instead of hiding from people, connection remains intact.

Relational rest sounds like:

• "I love you, but I need downtime tonight."

• "I need to recharge so I can show up well."

• "I'm emotionally tired — can we talk tomorrow?"

• "I'm not shutting down; I just need a breather."

The rhythm of rest prevents overgiving, overfunctioning, and overscheduling — three of the biggest contributors to emotional withdrawal.

Rest helps you:

• stay grounded

• stay connected

• stay emotionally regulated

• communicate without reacting

• maintain healthy boundaries

Without rest, relationships feel draining.

With rest, relationships feel sustainable.

Bible Reading

READ MATTHEW 11:28 (KJV)

Where are you overextending yourself relationally? Take some time to pray over this scripture with a heart that seeks God's will and clarity. Journal your thoughts and answers below.

Today's Challenge

Give yourself permission to rest today without guilt.

Every healthy relationship requires repair — not perfection.
You will misunderstand people.
People will misunderstand you.
But repair is what keeps connection from eroding.

Colossians 3:13 calls us to bear with one another — meaning, "be patient with each other's humanity."

The rhythm of repair includes:
· apologizing quickly
· extending grace
· clarifying miscommunications
· revisiting something calmly later
· choosing understanding over assumptions
· forgiving without keeping score
· remembering you're both human

Relationships don't end because of conflict — they end because of unrepaired conflict.
You don't repair connection by pretending everything is fine — you repair it by addressing issues with humility and compassion.

Repair sounds like:
· "I didn't mean for that to hurt you."
· "Can we talk about what happened?"
· "Help me understand your perspective."
· "I forgive you."
· "Thank you for being patient with me."

Repair keeps hearts soft.
Repair keeps communication clear.
Repair keeps relationships strong.

READ COLOSSIANS 3:13 (KJV)

Is there a relationship in your life that needs repair right now? Journal your thoughts below after reading and spending time in prayer.

Today's Challenge

Take one step — big or small — toward repairing something today.

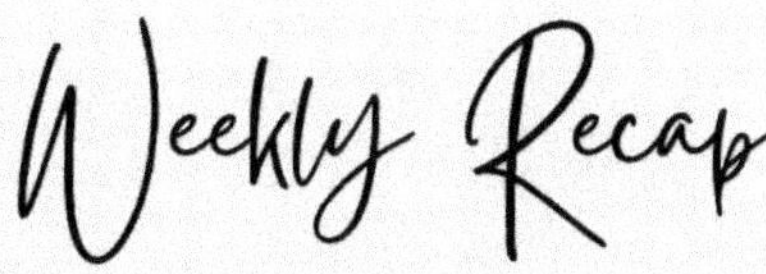

Weekly Recap

This week, you learned that relationships are strengthened through rhythm — not intensity. The more consistent your rhythms, the healthier your community becomes. You explored emotional presence, honest communication, rest, and relational repair — four rhythms that protect your heart and sustain connection long-term.

Reflect on what stood out:

· Which rhythm do you naturally lean into?

· Which rhythm do you need more practice with?

· How could emotional check-ins strengthen your connections?

· What truth have you avoided saying?

· Where do you need relational rest?

· What needs repairing before it becomes resentment?

You're not called to perfection — you're called to growth.
These rhythms won't only protect your relationships — they will protect you. They will keep you from withdrawing, overextending, shutting down, or slipping back into loneliness.

You are learning how to hold connection with grace, wisdom, and emotional maturity. And as you do, your relationships will become healthier, deeper, and more stable.

This week wasn't about doing more — it was about doing things differently.

Let this truth settle:
Healthy relationships are built through healthy rhythms — and you are learning them beautifully.

Weekly Prayer

Dear Father,

Thank you for teaching me the rhythms that strengthen connection.

Help me build habits of honesty, presence, rest, and repair.

Give me discernment to communicate with love, courage to be honest, and grace to navigate conflict.

Protect my relationships and guide me toward deeper, healthier connections.

Help me maintain these rhythms with consistency and joy.

Thank you for walking with me as I grow.

In Jesus' name,
Amen.

Week Seven

Day 1: Why You Need Guidance

You were not designed to grow alone. God uses mentors, spiritual mothers, leaders, and wise voices to guide your steps, shape your faith, and help you avoid unnecessary pain. Mentorship isn't a modern trend — it's God's pattern woven throughout Scripture.

Moses had Jethro.
Joshua had Moses.
Ruth had Naomi.
Elisha had Elijah.
Timothy had Paul.
The disciples had Jesus.

And you?
You, too, are meant to walk with someone who can see what you can't yet see.

Proverbs 11:14 teaches us that without guidance, people stumble. Guidance doesn't mean you're weak — it means you're wise. A mentor helps you:

· navigate emotional blind spots
· identify unhealthy patterns before they grow
· build spiritual maturity
· step confidently into purpose
· avoid repeating cycles
· stabilize your heart
· grow in ways you can't on your own

Loneliness often grows when you don't have someone spiritually grounded speaking into your life. But mentorship breaks isolation by anchoring you to wisdom, truth, and accountability.

You don't need a mentor because you're incapable — you need a mentor because God created growth to happen in relationship.

Bible Reading

READ PROVERBS 11:14 (KJV)

Spend time praying right now that God reveals to you where in your life guidance would bring clarity or stability? Journal your thoughts below.

Pray: "Lord, prepare the mentor You want to speak into my life."

Not every leader is a mentor. Not every older believer is spiritually mature. And not every relationship has the depth or alignment required for mentorship.
This is why Jesus teaches, "You will know them by their fruit."

A God-sent mentor carries fruit, not just knowledge.
They display:

· emotional maturity
· spiritual integrity
· consistency
· humility
· discernment
· healthy boundaries
· a life that reflects Christ

God-sent mentors don't control you — they guide you. They don't demand loyalty — they cultivate growth. They don't feed your dependence on them — they point you back to God.

A true mentor will:
· challenge you
· support you
· pray for you
· correct you with kindness
· celebrate your growth
· protect your confidentiality
· speak truth even when it's uncomfortable

Here's a secret:
Your mentor may not be someone you expected.
They may be older, younger, or simply further along in a specific area you're growing in.
Mentorship isn't about age — it's about fruit.

Look for fruit, not titles.
Look for character, not charisma.
Look for alignment, not popularity.

Bible Reading

READ MATTHEW 7:16 (KJV)

Read the scripture, then spend time in prayer asking
God to tell you what kind of "fruit" you want in the person
who mentors you.

Write the top 3 qualities you want in a mentor God sends.

You may not feel ready.
You may not feel qualified.
You may still be healing.
You may think someone else is better suited.

But hear me:
Your healing equips you.
Your story positions you.
Your growth has value.

Mentorship is not about perfection — it's about stewardship. God uses your experiences, mistakes, victories, and lessons to help someone who is where you once were.

2 Timothy 2:2 shows the pattern: someone poured into you, now you pour into others. Mentorship multiplies what God has done in your life.

You are qualified to mentor when:

- you've healed enough to speak from strength, not wounds
- you want to help without controlling
- you can listen without judgment
- you can encourage without rescuing
- you can guide without needing to be needed
- you point people to Jesus, not yourself
- you operate from humility, not authority

You don't need to have every answer — you just need a willing heart.

The enemy whispers, "Who do you think you are?"
God whispers, "You are who I healed you to become."

READ 2 TIMOTHY 2:2 (KJV)

Who in your life might God be nudging you to support or mentor? Take some time to pray over this scripture with a heart that seeks God's will and clarity. Journal your thoughts and answers below.

Ask God: "Make me a vessel of wisdom for someone in need."

Day 4 – Walking In Mentorship With Wisdom

Whether you are being mentored or mentoring someone else, wisdom and boundaries keep the relationship healthy. Without wisdom, mentorship becomes dependence. Without boundaries, it becomes draining.

Proverbs 4:7 reminds us to pursue wisdom above all — especially in relational roles.

Healthy mentorship means:
- clear communication
- emotional responsibility
- mutual respect
- protecting each other's humanity
- respecting time and capacity
- avoiding overattachment
- pointing each other toward Christ

Boundaries clarify expectations. They protect the relationship. They ensure the purpose stays pure.

If YOU are the one being mentored:
- communicate honestly
- show up consistently
- apply the wisdom given
- don't turn your mentor into your emotional crutch
- honor their time

If YOU are the mentor:
- set limits with love
- encourage independence
- keep God as the center
- avoid becoming their "rescuer"
- protect your emotional energy

Healthy mentorship has flow, not force.

READ PROVERBS 4:7 (KJV)

What boundary has been hard for you to maintain in past relationships? Journal your thoughts below after reading and spending time in prayer.

Create one clear boundary for your current or future mentorship relationships.

Weekly Recap

This week, you stepped into a deeper layer of connection — mentorship. You learned that God never designed spiritual growth to happen in isolation. You were created to be led by people ahead of you and to lead those who come after you.

Reflect on what God revealed:
- Where do you need guidance?
- What kind of mentor would support your next season?
- What fruit do you want in the people you follow?
- Who might God be preparing for you to mentor?
- Where do you need clearer boundaries?

Mentorship stabilizes your faith, accelerates your growth, and multiplies what God is doing in your life. It keeps you from slipping backward and helps you build emotional and spiritual strength that lasts.

You don't have to be perfect to step into mentorship — you just have to be willing, humble, and teachable. God uses ordinary people to lead extraordinary transformation.

This week wasn't about hierarchy — it was about heritage.
You are part of a lineage of belief, growth, and wisdom passed from generation to generation.

You are not walking alone — God is providing people to guide you, and He will use you to guide others.

Weekly Prayer

Dear Father,

Thank you for the gift of mentorship.

Send the right people to guide me and give me discernment to recognize their fruit.

Prepare my heart to mentor others with humility, wisdom, and grace.

Help me walk in healthy boundaries, emotional maturity, and spiritual clarity.

Teach me to lead like Jesus and follow with humility.

Strengthen the relationships You are building in my life and use them to shape me into who You've called me to be.

In Jesus' name,
Amen.

Week Eight

Loneliness is loud — but truth is louder.

If you want to sustain connection long-term, you must anchor yourself in truth every day. Because the lies you confronted in Week 3 don't disappear forever — they whisper again when you're tired, overwhelmed, triggered, or in transition.

Truth needs to be your daily anchor, not your occasional encouragement.

John 8:32 reminds us that truth sets you free — not once, but continually.
Truth frees your mind.
Truth frees your emotions.
Truth frees your relationships.

Daily truth looks like:
· reminding yourself you are chosen
· remembering you belong
· refusing shame-based thoughts
· choosing God's voice over fear
· reminding your heart that healing is real
· speaking identity over yourself

Truth is not a feeling — it's a spiritual discipline.
Because some days your heart will drift back into old lies. Some days you'll be tempted to withdraw. Some days you'll feel unworthy again.

That's why truth must become your rhythm. Your ritual. Your grounding.
Healing is sustained one truth-filled day at a time.

READ JOHN 8:32 (KJV)

Spend time praying right now that God reveal to you what truth you need to rehearse most consistently. Journal your thoughts below.

Choose one scripture about belonging and speak it over yourself every morning this week.

Once your heart begins to reopen, it must be maintained with intention.

Proverbs 4:23 tells you to guard your heart — not harden it. This means protecting what God has healed without slipping back into old patterns of overprotection, overthinking, or shutting down.

Your heart stays open through gentle, intentional choices:

· staying honest

· communicating early

· letting people know what you need

· sharing small parts of your day

· staying present instead of disappearing

· reminding yourself that vulnerability is strength

Healing doesn't close your heart — it strengthens it.

Healing teaches you how to stay open wisely, not recklessly.

You won't always feel like being open. Some days you'll prefer isolation because it feels easier or safer. But an open heart is a maintained heart.

Just like a muscle grows with use, connection grows with practice.

Your job isn't to be the most vulnerable person in the room.

Your job is simply to stay open enough for God to move — and for the right people to meet you where you are.

Bible Reading

READ PROVERBS 4:23 (KJV)

Read the scripture, then spend time in prayer asking God to reveal to you what makes you want to close your heart when connection gets uncomfortable. Write down ways which you can grow to be more connected with your community.

Choose one small moment of openness today — a text, a message, a conversation, or a truth shared.

Day 3 – Staying Connected to Community

Community fades quietly when consistency disappears.
You don't lose community in one big moment — you lose it through dozens of tiny moments of disconnection. Missed responses. Fewer check-ins. Longer silences. Busy weeks that turn into busy months.

Hebrews 10:24–25 calls us to continually encourage one another — because community must be nurtured to stay alive.

Daily connection doesn't require overwhelming energy or constant socializing. It simply requires consistency.
Small actions build big bonds.

Daily community rhythms include:
• sending one encouragement
• replying instead of disappearing
• sharing one honest thing
• asking one question
• joining one discussion
• showing up for five minutes
• praying for one friend

Connection thrives on small touches.
You don't need to be perfect — you just need to be present.

Over time, these small moments weave relational threads strong enough to hold your heart in seasons of stress, transition, or spiritual warfare.

You're not responsible for keeping every relationship alive — but you are responsible for maintaining intentional connection with the people God has highlighted in this season.

READ HEBREWS 10:24–25 (KJV)

Which connection in your life needs more consistent nurturing? Take some time to pray over this scripture with a heart that seeks God's will and clarity. Journal your thoughts and answers below.

Today's Challenge

Reach out to one person today with a genuine check-in or word of encouragement.

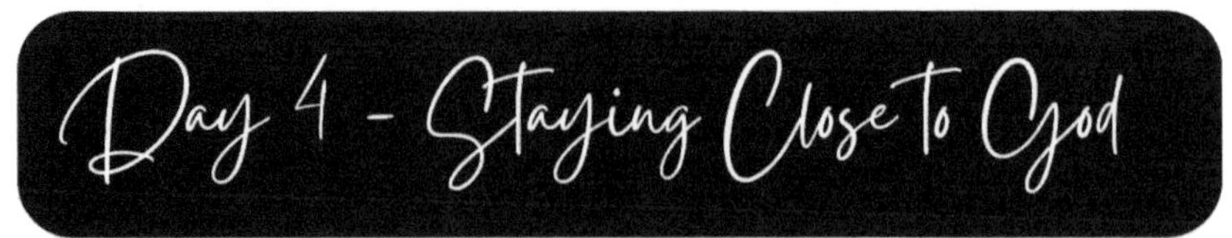

Human connection is powerful — but it cannot replace your connection with God. He is your anchor, your source, your stability, your comfort, your clarity, and your peace. Every other relationship flows from the quality of your relationship with Him.

James 4:8 offers a profound promise: if you draw near to God, He will draw near to you. Not might.
Not sometimes.
Will.

Your relationship with God sustains your connection with people by grounding you emotionally and spiritually.

Daily connection with God includes:
• prayer
• worship
• journaling
• reading His Word
• listening for His voice
• sitting quietly in His presence
• surrendering your day
• inviting Him into your emotions

The days you feel lonely — He is near.
The days you feel overwhelmed — He is present.
The days you feel unseen — He is watching.
The days you feel forgotten — He is calling your name.

Your connection with God is what keeps you from slipping back into isolation. When you are anchored in Him, you can connect with others from a place of security instead of fear.

Bible Reading

READ JAMES 4:8 (KJV)

Which daily practice strengthens your connection
with God the most? Journal your thoughts below
after reading and spending time in prayer.

Today's Challenge

Spend 10 intentional minutes with God today — fully present,
fully open.

Weekly Recap

This week was the final step in learning how to live out the healing God has done in your heart. You discovered the daily rhythms that sustain connection, protect your emotional life, and anchor you spiritually.
You've learned truth, openness, consistency, and anchored intimacy with God — the four pillars of ongoing relational health.

Reflect on your journey:
· What truth has set you free the most?
· Where has your heart remained open in moments you would've closed before?
· Which small connections have strengthened your community?
· How has your intimacy with God deepened through this process?
· What rhythms do you want to carry forward into the next season?

You are not the same woman who started this study.
You've uprooted lies, confronted wounds, built trust, restored connection, found alignment, established rhythms, and begun stepping into mentorship.

You've grown.
You've softened.
You've matured.
You've healed.

And now you're walking with confidence, clarity, and connection into a life God-designed — not loneliness-defined.

Let this truth settle over you:
You are never alone.
You never were.
And you never will be again.

Weekly Prayer

Dear Father,

Thank you for walking with me through this entire journey.

Seal this healing in my heart. Help me walk daily in truth, openness, connection, and intimacy with You.

Strengthen every rhythm I've learned and guide me into a life of lasting community and deep relationships.

Keep my heart soft, my mind clear, and my spirit anchored in Your presence.

Thank You for surrounding me with Your love and preparing a future full of connection.

In Jesus' name,
Amen.

Sweet Sister,

I want you to pause and recognize something holy: You're not the same woman who started this journey.

You've told the truth about your loneliness. You've faced the patterns that kept you isolated. You've let God speak into places you once guarded tightly. And you've taken brave steps toward connection, healing, and belonging.

I know what it feels like to carry life alone. I know the silence, the ache, the self-protection, the exhaustion. But I also know this: God never designed you to walk alone — and He certainly didn't start with you.

You were created for community that strengthens you. Friendships that feel like home. Sisterhood that lifts your arms when life gets heavy. And a spiritual family that sees you, knows you, and walks with you.

If this study stirred something in you...
If you're craving connection...
If you're ready to build real relationships...

I want to personally invite you into two communities built exactly for that:

Mission Driven Sisters: A global sisterhood for women who want authentic friendship, support, growth, and faith-filled conversations. Join us at MissionDrivenSisters.com.

Mission Driven Church: An online group of believers focused on living out their faith — including small groups, prayer, teaching, and a family that actually walks life with you. Visit us at MissionDrivenChurch.com to learn more.

You don't have to pretend.
You don't have to isolate to feel safe.
You don't have to be strong alone.

There is a place for you — a real one.

And it's waiting.

I am so proud of you.

And I cannot wait to see the relationships God brings into your life as you continue rising.

With love, strength, and sisterhood,
Bridget Irby

Continue Your Journey Toward Freedom

What you've just worked through is only one part of a bigger story.

The *You Are Not Called* series was created to help Christian women break free from the emotional struggles that quietly keep them stuck—often beneath the surface of faith, responsibility, and strength.

Each book in the series focuses on a different area where many women feel trapped, overwhelmed, or disconnected, including anger, anxiety, loneliness, fear, and shame.

While each study can be read on its own, the greatest transformation often happens when these truths are layered together over time.

If this book resonated with you, you're not alone—and you don't have to stop here.

The *You Are Not Called* Series

Continue your journey with the other studies in the series:

You Are Not Called to Be Angry
A Bible Study for Christian Women Ready to Break Free from Anger

You Are Not Called to Be Anxious
A Bible Study for Christian Women Ready to Break Free from Anxiety

You Are Not Called to Be Alone
A Bible Study for Christian Women Ready to Break Free from Loneliness

You Are Not Called to Be Afraid
A Bible Study for Christian Women Ready to Break Free from Fear

You Are Not Called to Be Ashamed
A Bible Study for Christian Women Ready to Break Free from Shame

Each book builds on the biblical truth about who you are and your calling — helping you heal deeply, renew your mind, and walk forward in the freedom God has always intended for you.

A Final Word Before You Go

You don't have to rush this process. Healing is not a race—it's a relationship.

As you continue through the series, allow God to meet you where you are, speak truth into the places that feel tender, and gently lead you forward. You are not behind. You are not broken. And you are not alone on this journey.

God has more for you—and freedom is closer than you think.

Free Resources

Hey there, superstar!

You've made it through the book, and I'm so proud of you. But let's be real - reading is just the first step. Now it's time to put all this good stuff into practice. And because I'm not about to send you out there empty-handed, I've got some awesome resources to help you on your journey.

Think of these as your anger management toolkit. They're like the Swiss Army knife of emotional growth - versatile, handy, and they might just save you in a pinch (though maybe don't try to use them to open a can or cut down a small tree).

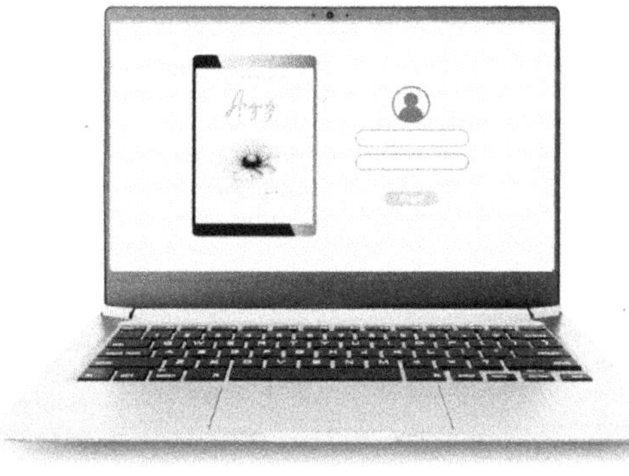

To access the resources, simply create your free account at www.youarenotcalled.com.

Inside, you'll have to the above resources plus much more!